Lightning-fast

FRENCH

FOR KIDS AND FAMILIES

Learn French, speak French, teach kids French — even if you don't speak a word now!

- Built around every day situations – no need to set aside special time, and you will use your new language the first day!

- Phonetic pronunciation included – no current French knowledge needed!

- Fun and easy to start!

Contents

Introduction

Like so many others, this story starts when I had children. I had been ineffectively learning Spanish for 20+ years (never got much past "mas tacos por favor"). Once the children started arriving I was focused for several years on bottles, diapers, and trying to catch up on my sleep. But once they got into school and I had a little time to read again I learned that kids who are bilingual are supposed to have an edge in life. I of course wanted the best for my crew, so I began obsessively buying language programs and trying them out on my too-young-to-complain subjects.

After a year or so of this, I was burned out with the whole concept, and my kids had pretty much achieved the ability to count to 10 in Spanish. But still I encouraged them to press on. "If we can just get to the point where we can speak to each other in Spanish, I think it will all start to come together for us! We can practice around the house, and then get comfortable enough to try it with outsiders".

And then, the light bulb finally came on. Instead of waiting for us to gain the ability to talk to each other, perhaps I could pay attention to the things we talk about, translate them into Spanish, write them down – and we could start talking to each other in Spanish right away!

Once we started using the Spanish book we got even more inspired – and I had the conversations translated into several more languages my kids wanted to learn.

And so, this book was born. We have had a lot of fun putting these together and using them, and have actually learned some foreign languages along the way.

Now it's your turn! Jump in and try them!

Grammar notes

I don't believe you need to know grammar to speak French; that will come to you as you learn and use words in context. But these are a few items that I think will help you avoid confusion as you go through the scenarios to follow…

Grammar note #1: gender

You probably are already aware that French nouns have "gender", and the articles (a, an, the) put before them must reflect that gender. The choice of male vs. female is not always obvious to a native English speaker, so it's important to keep the article with the word when you are memorizing it.

In terms of usage – the words will be shown with la (feminine) or le (masculine), these words mean "the". To switch to "a" – use une (feminine) or un (masculine).

** This is not something to spend lots of time worrying about – once you get enough French to converse with native speakers your pronunciation and grammar will improve rapidly. If you say a few of these things incorrectly at the beginning they will understand.

Grammar note #2: word order

In many cases word order in French is the same as in English – but one exception is that adjectives generally follow the nouns they describe. So, "the red house" in English would become "la maison rouge" , or "the house red", in French.

How to use this book

The fastest way to learn French is to use it! If you want your family to speak French you need to find ways to incorporate it into your everyday life.

I found the biggest obstacle to teaching my children a foreign language was time. I don't speak the language, so in order to teach I would have to first research and memorize. Somehow that just never happened.

This program is designed to eliminate that obstacle. To get started, identify a time of day or daily conversation that you think would be easiest to start with. Although the conversations are numbered one through fifteen you do not need to use them in that order. If there are particular activities or times of day that seem easier to add French to, start there. They are intended to be stand-alone, with any needed vocabulary repeated, with the exception of #15 - which is a recap of all prior lessons.

Turn to the appropriate section of the book and jump in! Any suggested preparation is noted at the beginning of the section, and there are example sentences to use right away. There are also additional vocabulary lists in each section so you can tailor the sentences to your specific situation.

Start off the conversation by reading a sentence, and acting it out as much as you can. For example, hold up a red skirt and some black pants, and ask, "Préfères-tu - la jupe rouge ou le pantalon noir?" (Pray-fair-uh-ray tew met-ruh la jhew-puh rou-jhuh oo luh pahn-ta-lohn nwar?)- "Which do you prefer – the red skirt or the black pants?" Shake or point to the skirt when you say "jupe", and to the pants when you say "pantalon".

Your student will probably look at you blankly. In that case, say in English, "I'm asking you which you prefer, the red skirt or the black pants". Then, repeat the question in French: "Préfères-tu - la jupe rouge ou le pantalon noir?"

They will likely now point to one or the other. This is your queue to feed them the reply you'd like – for example, say "Can you say it in French? La jupe rouge?" and wait for them to repeat it. The act of speaking and the visual of you holding up the red skirt will help them remember the words.

That only took about 10 seconds! Just a few minutes each day built around visual cues and daily activities will start building your French skills.

One key to remember is that you will need to use each conversation a few times before the vocabulary becomes second nature. Rather than trying to go through the entire book at once, plan on introducing one or two conversations a week and repeat each a few times. You can start with just a few of the vocabulary words the first time through, and add a few more each time you repeat it.

You will find after a few repetitions that you won't need the notes any more, and that you and your students will be able to "ad lib" a bit.

Once you reach this point it would be good to expose your group to native speakers. Don't worry if your vocabulary is limited, most people will be happy to help you! Being around people speaking French in context will improve your skills faster than any amount of flash cards or DVDs.

It can be scary the first time you use your new French language skills in public. One way to dip your toe in the water would be to eat in a French restaurant, with a goal of communicating with your server in French. The vocabulary in the "What's for dinner" and "What's for lunch" sections will easily translate to a restaurant setting.

As a next step, so you might try going to a park or playground in an area where many native speakers live. If you have passed #9 "Want to Play" you will probably find that your children bravely walk up to other children and ask them, "Salut! Veux-tu jouer?" That's your queue to say "Salut!" to the parents as well!

The back section of the book includes fun games and activities that you can use to reinforce the French you are learning. Plug them into your study at any time you feel ready for them.

Now it's time for the most crucial step – getting started! Go ahead, pick a section, and start learning French Lightning-Fast!

Conversation #1:   Getting dressed

Concepts / vocabulary introduced:

Names of clothing items
Colors
Adjectives

Preparation:

Get out a selection of clothing. Alternatively – you can start with a basket of clothes you need to sort out and get two things done at once!

The Conversation:

You will hold up two different items of clothing, and ask questions. Here are several different questions to get you started:

Lequel aimes-tu le plus? (luh-kel em tew luh plews) - Which do you like better?

Lequel est à toi? (luh-kel et-ta twa) - Which one is yours?

Préfères-tu XXX ou XXX? (Pray-fair tew XXX oo XXX) - Do you prefer XXX or XXX?

Préférerais-tu mettre XXX ou XXX? (Pray-fair-uh-ray tew met-ruh XXX oo XXX) - Would you rather wear the XXX or XXX?

Est-ce que c'est rouge ou bleu? (Ess-kuh say rou-jhuh oo bloo) – Is this red or blue?

You will want to describe the objects you are holding up as part of the question. For example, I might hold up a red skirt and some black pants. I could ask my daughter, "Lequel est à toi : la jupe rouge ou le pantalon

noir?" (luh-kel et-ta twa : la jhew-puh rou-jhuh oo luh pahn-ta-lohn nwar?)
- "Which is yours – the red skirt or the black pants?"

When your students have memorized some of the words, you can move on to holding up a single item and ask, "Qu'est-ce que c'est? " (Kes-kuh say) - "What is this?" They should then answer with, "C'est XXX" (say XXX) where they include some specifics about the item, for example "C'est une jupe rouge" (Set-tewn jhew-puh roo-jhuh)– "It's a red skirt".

Vocabulary:

Clothing:

la blouse (la bloo-zuh) - blouse
le manteau (luh mahn-toe) - coat
la robe (la rob-buh) - dress
le chapeau (luh sha-po) - hat
le veston (luh ves-tohn) - jeacket
le jean (luh djeen) - jeans
le pyjama (luh pijh-am-ah) - pajamas
le pantalon (luh pahn-ta-lohn) – pants, trousers
le sac à main (luh sak a mayhn) - purse
la chemise (la shuh-mee-zuh) - shirt
le soulier (luh soo-lee-ay) - shoe
le short (luh short) - shorts
la jupe (la jhew-puh) - skirt
la chaussette (la sho-set-tuh) - sock
le chandail (luh shahn-dye) - sweater
le chandail en coton molletonné (luh shahn-dye ahn kot-tohn mol-ton-nay) - sweatshirt
le costume de bain (luh kos-tewm duh bayhn) - swimsuit
les sous-vêtements (leh soo-vayt-mahn) - underwear

Colors:

jaune (jho-nuh) - yellow
bleu (bluh) - blue
beige (bay-jhuh) - beige
blanc (blahn) – white (masculine noun)
blanche (blahn-shuh) – white (feminine noun)
bourgogne (boor-goyng-yuh) - burgundy
gris (gree) – gray (masculine noun)
grise (gree-zuh) – gray (feminine noun)
brun (bruhn) – brown (masculine noun)
brune (brew-nuh) – brown (feminine noun)
pourpre (poor-pruh) - purple
orange (oh-rahn-jhuh) - orange
noir (nwar) - black
rouge (roo-jhuh) - red
rose (ro-zuh) - pink
vert (vair) – green (masculine noun)
verte (vair-tuh) – green (feminine noun)
turquoise (tur-kwah-zuh) - aqua

Adjectives:

long (lohn) – long (masculine noun)
longue (lohn-guh) – long (feminine noun)
court (koor) – short (masculine noun)
courte (koor-tuh) – short (feminine noun)
rayé (ray-ay) - striped
écossais (ay-koss-ay) – plaid (masculine noun)
ecossaise (ay-koss-ay-zuh) – plaid (feminine noun)
imprimé (ahm-pree-may) - patterned

Conversation #2: What's for breakfast?

Concepts / vocabulary introduced:

>Foods and descriptors
>Numbers one to five

Preparation:

Get out some breakfast food items. The vocabulary list includes eggs, bread, toast, bacon, butter, jelly, waffles, muffins, bananas, yogurt and orange juice.

The Conversation:

First, let everyone know that:

>J'aimerais (jhem-uh-ray) = I would like, a polite way of asking for something

>Aimerais-tu (em-uh-ray tew) = Would you like?

>Oui (wee) = Yes

>Non merci (no mair-see) = No thank you

>Encore (ahn-kor) = More

Then for each person, stand by the choices holding their plate. You will ask them if they want something, and they will say yes or no.

For example, if you have waffles, ask "Aimerais-tu une gauffre? " (em-uh-ray tew ewn go-fruh)

They answer either "Oui, j'aimerais une gauffre. " (Wee, jhem-uh-ray ewn go-fruh), or ""No merci, pas de gauffre" (no mair-see, pah duh go-fruh). Once you put it on their plate, ask if they would like more: "Aimerais-tu encore des gauffres? " (em-uh-ray tew ahn-kor day go-fruh) And they can again answer, "Oui j'aimerais encore des gauffres. " (Wee, jhem-uh-ray ahn-kor day go-fruh), or "Non merci. " (No mair-see).

Some other sentences that may be useful:

Qu'est-ce qu'on mange pour le petit déjeuner? (Kes-kohn mahnjh poor luh puh-tee day-jhuh-nay) - What are we having for breakfast?

J'aimerais XXX pour le petit déjeuner. (Jhem-uh-ray XXX poor luh puh-tee day-jhuh-nay) - I would like XXX for breakfast.

J'aimerais plus de XXX s'il te plait. (Jhem-uh-ray plews duh XXX sil tuh play) - I would like more XXX please

Combien en aimerais-tu? (Kohm-byehn ahn nem-uh-ray tew) - How many would you like?

J'aimerais trois de plus s'il te plait. (Jhem-uh-ray trwa duh plews, sil tuh play) – I would like three more XXX please

Vocabulary:

Polite requests:

J'aimerais (jhem-uh-ray) = I would like, a polite way of asking
Aimerais-tu (em-uh-ray tew) = Would you like?
Oui (wee) = Yes
Non merci (no mair-see) = No thank you

Numbers:

Un (uhn) - one
Deux (doo) - two
Trois (trwa) - three
Quatre (kat-ruh) - four
Cinq (sahnk) - five

Food list:

Des oeufs (day-zuh) - Eggs
Des oeufs brouillés (day-zuh broo-yay) – Scrambled eggs
Bacon (bay-kon) - Bacon
Rôtie (ro-tee) - Toast
Pain (payhn) - Bread
Tranches de pain (trahn-shuh duh payhn) – Pieces of bread
Beurre (buh-rruh) - Butter
Confiture (kohn-fee-tew-ruh) - Jelly
Confiture aux fraises (kohn-fee-tew-ruh oh fray-zuh) – Strawberry jelly
Une gauffre (ewn-nuh go-fruh) - Waffle
Des gauffres (day go-fruh)- Waffles
Sirop (see-ro) - Syrup
Muffin (muf-fin) - Muffin
Banane (ba-nan-nuh) - Banana
In Québec : Yogourt (yo-goor) In France : Yaourt (ya-oort) - Yogurt
Jus d'orange (jhew dor-ahn-jhuh) – Orange juice

Conversation #3:   Ready to go?

Concepts / vocabulary introduced:

> Getting dressed
> Brushing hair
> Packing lunch

Preparation:

This role play takes place just before you leave the house, so leave some extra time!

The Conversation:

You will ask if each task is completed while imitating it. By this time they should respond either "oui" or "non". You will then need to feed them the appropriate full sentence answer. For example, you might say T-es-tu brossé les dents? (Tay-tew bros-say lay dahn) - Have you brushed your teeth? while making a teeth-brushing motion with your hand. The child might answer "Oui" or "non", or might answer "yes" or "no" in English. If they look confused, say "I am asking if you have brushed your teeth yet", and then repeat the question in French again. Once they have answered, feed them the entire answer sentence in French – either "Oui, je me suis brossé les dents" (Wee, jhuh muh swee bros-say lay dahn)
 or "Non, je ne me suis pas brossé les dents" (No, jhuh nuh muh swee pah bros-say lay dahn),and have them repeat it.

It may feel a bit slow and cumbersome the first time through, but if you repeat a few mornings in a row it will quickly become easy.

Here are question and possible answer combinations:

Bonjour! Es-tu prêt (fem . : prête) à partir? (Bohn-jhoor! Ay-tew pray (fem. : pret-tuh) a par-teer?) - Good morning! Are you ready to go?
Oui, je suis prêt (fem . : prête) à partir. (Wee, jhuh swee pray (fem. : prêt-tuh) a par-teer) - Yes, I am ready to go
Non, je ne suis pas prêt (fem . : prête) à partir. (No, jhuh nuh swee pah pray (fem.: prêt-tuh) a par-teer) - No, I am not ready to go

T-es-tu brossé les dents? (Tay-tew bros-say lay dahn) - Have you brushed your teeth?
Oui, je me suis brossé les dents. (Wee, jhuh muh swee bros-say lay dahn) - Yes, I have brushed my teeth
Non, je ne me suis pas brossé les dents. (No, jhuh nuh muh swee pah bros-say lay dahn) - No, I have not brushed my teeth

T'es-tu brossé les cheveux? (Tay-tew bros-say lay shuh-voo) - Have you brushed your hair?
Oui, je me suis brossé les cheveux. (Wee, jhuh muh swee bros-say lay shuh-voo) – Yes, I have brushed my hair
Non, je me suis pas brossé les cheveux. (No, jhuh nuh muh swee pah bros-say lay shuh-voo) – No, I have not brushed my hair

As-tu préparé ton déjeuner ? (Ah-tew pray-pa-ray tohn day-jhuh-nay?) - Have you prepared your lunch?
Oui, j'ai préparé mon déjeuner . (Wee, jhay pray-pa-ray mohn day-jhuh-nay) - Yes, I have prepared my lunch
Non, je n'ai pas préparé mon déjeuner . (No, jhuh nay pah pray-pa-ray mohn day-jhuh-nay) – No, I have not prepared my lunch

Es-tu habillé ? (Eh-tew ab-bee-ay ?) - Are you dressed?
Oui, je suis habillé. (Wee, jhuh swee ab-bee-ay) - Yes, I am dressed
Non, je ne suis pas habillé. (No, jhuh nuh swee pah ab-bee-ay) – No, I am not dressed

Portes-tu XXX ? (port-tew XXX) – Are you wearing XXX?
Oui, je porte XXX. (Wee, jhuh port XXX) – Yes, I am wearing XXX
Non, je ne porte pas XXX. (No, jhuh nuh port pah XXX) – No, I am not wearing XXX

Here are examples with some specific clothing items filled in:

Portes-tu une chemise ? (port-tew ewn-nuh shuh-mee-zuh) - Are you wearing a shirt?

Portes-tu un pantalon ? (port-tew uhn pahn-ta-lohn) - Are you wearing pants?

Portes-tu des souliers ? (port-tew day soo-lee-ay) - Are you wearing shoes?

Portes-tu des chaussettes ? (port-tew day sho-set-tuh) - Are you wearing socks?

Portes-tu une robe ? (port-tew ewn-nuh rob-buh) - Are you wearing a dress?

Conversation #4:   Where are we going?

Concepts / vocabulary introduced:

Names of places
J'ai besoin de (jhay buh-zwahn duh), or "I need"
Nous avons besoin de (noo za-vohn buh-zwahn duha), or "we need"
Aller (al-lay), or "to go"
Words relating to timing of events

Preparation:

Think about the errands or stops you need to make.

The Conversation:

First, discuss your errands. Start with, "Nous avons besoin d'aller à" (noo za-vohn buh-zwahn dal-lay a) - We need to go to – and name places to go.

Examples:
Premièrement, nous avons besoin d'aller à l'épicerie (Pruh-myair-uh-mahn noo za-vohn buh-zwahn dal-lay a lay-pee-suh-ree) – First, we need to go to the grocery store.
Plus tard, nous avons besoin d'aller à la bibliothèque (Plew tar, noo za-vohn buh-zwahn dal-lay a la bee-blee-oh-tek) – Later, we need to go to the library.
Nous avons besoin d'aller à l'école bientôt. (Noo za-vohn buh-zwahn dal-lay a lay-kol-luh bee-ehn-toe) – We need to go to the school soon.

Have your students repeat back the planned errands, and make sure they understand what they are saying.

You can then move into some proposed other stops:

Veux-tu aller au terrain de jeu aussi ? (Voo-tew al-lay oh tair-rayhn duh joo oh-see) – Would you like to go to the playground too?

Once the plan is complete – say "Allons à la voiture" (al-lohn a la vwa-tew-ruh) – Let's go to the car!

Vocabulary:

Timing of events:

Aujourd'hui (oh-joor-dwee) - Today
Demain (duh-mayhn) - Tomorrow
Plus tard (Plew tar) - Later
Maintenant (mayhn-tuh-nahn) - Now
Bientôt (bee-ehn-toe) - Soon
La semaine prochaine (la suh-men prosh-en-nuh) – Next week
Dans une semaine (Dahn zewn suh-men-nuh) – In a week
Premier (pruh-mee-ay) - First
Deuxième (doo-zee-em-muh) - Second
Troisième (trwa-zee-em-muh) - Third
Quatrième (kat-ree-em-muh) - Fourth
Aussi (oh-see) - Also

Places to go:

L'école (lay-kol-luh) - School
L'église (lay-glee-zuh) - Churck
La maison de XXX (la may-zohn duh XXX) – XXX's house
Le magasin (luh mag-ga-zayhn) - Store
L'épicerie (lay-pee-suh-ree) – Grocery store
La quincaillerie (la kayhn-kye-uh-ree) – Hardware store
Le magasin à rayons (luh mag-ga-zayhn a ray-ohn) – Department store
Le parc (luh park) - Park
Le terrain de jeux (luh tair-rayhn duh joo) - Playground
La piscine (la pee-seen) – Swimming pool
La gymnase (la jhim-nahz-zuh) - Gym
La librairie (la lee-brair-ree) - Library
Le poste d'essence (luh poss-tuh dess-ahn-suh) – Gas station

Conversation #5:   Comparisons / opposites

Concepts / vocabulary introduced:

Comparison words

Preparation:

Not many object names have been covered yet, so this role play works best if you walk around the house and find appropriate comparisons. You will provide the comparisons, but not try to name the objects.

The Conversation:

Walk around the house, and look for objects to compare. First you will show the comparison, and then ask the child(ren) to imitate it, as they will learn much faster if they say it themselves.

Here are suggestions:
- Go into the bathroom. Point to a wet towel (or get out a washcloth and wet it), and say "Mouillé". Point to a dry towel and say "Sec".
- Go into a child's bedroom. Point to a stuffed toy and say "Doux". Rap your knuckle on the bed frame and say "Dur".
- Go into the kitchen, and fill a glass with water. Say "Plein", then empty the water into the sink, hold the glass up again and say "Vide".
- Point to yourself, and then hold your hand horizontally at the top of your head. Say "grand" if you are a man, "grande" if you are a woman. Hold your hand horizontally at the height of your child's head, and say "petit" (for a boy) or "petite" (for a girl). (This only works if they are shorter than you! If not you can compare yourself to a pet or to some other shorter item)

- Point to your face, and make a big smile Say "heureux". Then, make a very sad face and say "triste".
- Pull a large cooking spoon out, and say "long". Then pull out a teaspoon and say "court".
- Go into the living room. Point to the sofa and say "gros". Then, point to a small object like a block, and say "petit".
- Locate 2 toy vehicles. Drive one quickly along the floor and say "vite". Drive the second slowly, and say "lent".
- Open a chest or box, or a door, and say "ouvert". Close it, and say "fermé".

Vocabulary:

Long (lohn) – long (masculine noun)
Longue (lohn-guh) – long (feminine noun)
Court (koor) – short (masculine noun)
Courte (koor-tuh) – short (feminine noun)
Clair (clair) - light
Foncé (fohn-say) - dark
Gros (gro) – tall (masculine noun)
Grosse (gro-suh) – tall (feminine noun)
Petit (puh-tee) – short (masculine noun)
Petite (puh-tee-tuh) – short (feminine noun)
Grand (grahn) – big (masculine noun)
Grande (grahn-duh) – big (feminine noun)
Petit (puh-tee) – small (masculine noun)
Petite (puh-tee-tuh) – small (feminine noun)
Joli (jhol-lee) - pretty
Laid (lay) – ugly (masculine noun)
Laide (led-duh) – ugly (feminine noun)
Heureux (oo-roo) – happy (masculine noun)
Heureuse (oo-roo-zuh) – happy (feminine noun)
Triste (treess-tuh) - sad
Plein (playhn) – full (masculine noun)
Pleine (plen-nuh) – full (feminine noun)
Vide (veed) - empty
Mouillé (moo-yay) - wet
Sec (sek) – dry (masculine noun)
Sèche (sesh-uh) – dry (feminine noun)

Vite (veet) - fast
Lent (lahn) – slow (masculine noun)
Lente (lahn-tuh) – slow (feminine noun)
En haut (ahn oh) - up
En bas (ahn bah)down
Épais (ay-pay) – thick (masculine noun)
Épaisse (ay-pess-suh) – thick (feminine noun)
Mince (mayhn-suh) - thin
Doux (doo) – soft (masculine noun)
Douce (doo-suh) – soft (feminine noun)
Dur (dewr) - hard
Ouvert (oo-vair) – open (masculine noun)
Ouverte (oo-vair-tuh) – open (feminine noun)
Fermé (fair-may) - closed

Conversation #6:   My toys

Concepts / vocabulary introduced:

Names of different objects
Continued practice on colors and comparison words

Preparation:

Select several toys to use for the role play, and make sure you know the
French name for each of them.

The Conversation:

First, introduce the objects you will be using. For example, hold up a toy
train and say,
C'est un train (set-tuhn trayhn)

Once you've introduced several objects, ask questions and have the
student point to or pick up the item you are asking about:
Regarde le train (ruh-gar-duh luh trayhn) – Look for the train
Vois-tu le train ? (vwa-tew luh trayhn) – Do you see the train ?
Je vois un train (jhuh vwa uhn trayhn) – I see a train
Je vois un train rouge (jhuh vwa uhn trayhn roo-jhuh) – I see a red train
Lequel est le train ? (luh-kel ay luh trayhn) – Which is the train ?

Vocabulary:

Regarde (ruh-gar-duh) – Look for
Vois-tu (vwa-tew) – Do you see
Je vois (jhuh vwa) – I see
Lequel est (luh-kel ay) – Which is
Le train (luh trayhn) the train

L a voiture (la vwah-tew-ruh) – the car
L'hélicoptère (lay-lee-cop-tair-ruh) – the helicopter
L'avion (la-vee-ohn) – the airplane
La poupée (la poo-pay) – the doll
La balle (la bal-luh) – the ball
Le livre (luh lee-vruh) – the book
Le camion (luh cam-yohn) – the truck
Le camion de pompiers (luh cam-yohn duh pom-pyay) – the firetruck
L'ours (loorss) – the bear
Le tambour (luh tahm-boor) – the drum
Le bloc (luh blok) – the block

More colors:

Jaune (jho-nuh) - yellow
Bleu (bloo) – blue (masculine noun)
Beige (bay-jhuh) – blue (feminine noun)
Blanc (blahn) – white (masculine noun)
Blanche (blahn-shuh) – white (feminine noun)
Bourgogne (boor-goyng-yuh) - burgundy
Café (caf-fay) - brown
Cannelle (can-nel-luh) - tan
Doré (dor-ray) - gold
Émeraude (ay-muh-ro-duh) - emerald
Gris (gree) – gray (masculine noun)
Grise (gree-zuh) – gray (feminine noun)
Lavande (la-vahn-duh) - lavender
Magenta (ma-jhahn-tah) - magenta
Marron (ma-rohn) - brown
Pourpre (poor-pruh) - purple
Orange (or-rahn-jhuh) - orange
Noir (nwar) - black
Argenté (ar-jhahn-tay) - silver
Rouge (roo-jhuh) - red
Rose (ro-zuh) - pink
Turquoise (tur-kwah-zuh) - turquoise
Vert (vair) – green (masculine noun)
Verte (vair-tuh) – green (feminine noun)
Vert aqua (vair ak-kwa) - aqua

<u>Refresher – comparisons:</u>

Long (lohn) – long (masculine noun)
Longue (lohn-guh) – long (feminine noun)
Court (koor) – short (masculine noun)
Courte (koor-tuh) – short (feminine noun)
Grand (grahn) – big (masculine noun)
Grande (grahn-duh) – big (feminine noun)
Petit (puh-tee) – small (masculine noun)
Petite (puh-tee-tuh) – small (feminine noun)
Joli (jhol-lee) - pretty
Laid (lay) – ugly (masculine noun)
Laide (led-duh) – ugly (feminine noun)
Plein (playhn) – full (masculine noun)
Pleine (plen-nuh) – full (feminine noun)
Vide (veed) - empty
Mouillé (moo-yay) - wet
Sec (sek) – dry (masculine noun)
Sèche (sesh-uh) – dry (feminine noun)
Vite (veet) - fast
Lent (lahn) – slow (masculine noun)
Lente (lahn-tuh) – slow (feminine noun)
En haut (ahn oh) - up
En bas (ahn bah)down
Doux (doo) – soft (masculine noun)
Douce (doo-suh) – soft (feminine noun)
Dur (dewr) - hard

Conversation #7: What's for lunch?

Concepts / vocabulary introduced:

Foods and descriptors

Preparation:

Set out ingredients to make sandwiches, and also some fruit or carrots if you have them available. Also set out some plates and silverware.

The Conversation:

First, teach a few statements that will be used regularly going forward:
Qu'est-ce qu'on mange pour le déjeuner ? (Kes-kohn mahnjh poor luh day-jhuh-nay) - What are we having for lunch?
J'aimerais XXX pour le déjeuner. (Jhem-uh-ray XXX poor luh day-jhuh-nay) - I would like XXX for lunch

Then for the role play, explain that they will each be putting together their own sandwich. They will need to ask for each ingredient they need.

"Passe-moi XXX, s'il te plaît. " (pass-mwah XXX, sil tuh play) – Please pass the XXX
"Voilà XXX" (vwah-la XXX)– Here is the XXX

Vocabulary:

<u>Refresher:</u>

J'aimerais (jhem-uh-ray) = I would like, a polite way of asking
Aimerais-tu (em-uh-ray tew) = Would you like?
Oui (wee) = Yes
Non merci (no mair-see) = No thank you

<u>Food list:</u>

Le pain (luh payhn) - bread
Le pain de blé (luh payhn duh blay) – wheat bread
Le pain blanc (luh payhn blahn) – white bread
La mayonnaise (la may-on-nayz) - mayonnaise
La moutarde (la moo-tard) - mustard
La dinde (la dayhn-duh) - turkey
Le fromage (luh fro-ma-jhuh) - cheese
Le fromage cheddar (luh fro-ma-jh shed-ar) – cheddar cheese
Le fromage suisse (luh fro-ma-jh swiss) – swiss cheese
Le sandwich (luh sahn-dwish) - sandwich
La pomme (la pomm) - apple
L'orange (lor-ahn-jhuh) - orange
La banane (la ba-nan-uh) - banana
Les fraises (lay fraze-uh) - strawberries
Les bleuets (lay bloo-ay) (Québec), Les myrtes (lay meer-tuh) (France) - blueberries
Les carottes (lay ca-rot) - carrots
L'assiette (lass-yet) - plate
Le couteau (luh coo-toe) - knife

Conversation #8:   A walk outside

Concepts / vocabulary introduced:

Names of items you will see in a walk around the block

Preparation:

None! Just your vocabulary lists if you need them at hand.

The Conversation:

For this role play you will just take a walk and point out things you see. You and the students can incorporate comparison words and colors into your discussion.

Here are some examples:

C'est une clôture. (Say-tewn clo-tew-ruh) – This is a fence.
De quelle couleur est la clôture ? (De kel coo-loor ay la clo-tew-ruh?) – What color is the fence?
La clôture est rouge. (La clo-tew-ruh ay roo-jhuh) – The fence is red.
Vois-tu une roche ? (Vwah-tew ew-nuh rosh-uh?) – Do you see a rock ?
Est-ce que la roche est grosse ou petite ? (Ess-kuh la rosh ay gro-suh oo puh-tee-tuh?) – Is the rock big or small ?
La roche est petite. (La rosh ay puh-tee-tuh) – The rock is small.
Est-ce que l'herbe est longue ou petite ? (Ess-kuh lair-buh ay lohn-guh oo koor-tuh?) – Is the grass long or short?
L'herbe est longue. (Lair-buh ay lohn-guh) – The grass is long.

Vocabulary:

L'arbre (Lahr-bruh) - Tree
La fleur (La floor) - Flower
Les fleurs (lay floor) - Flowers
L'arbuste (Lahr-bews-tuh) - Bush
L'herbe (Lair-buh) – Grass
La roche (La rosh-uh) - Rock
La terre (La tair-ruh)Dirt
Le papillon (Luh pap-ee-yohn) - Butterfly
Le scarabée (Le sca-ra-bay) - Beetle
La fourmi (La foor-mee) - Ant
L'oiseau (Lwah-zo) - Bird
L'écureuil (Lay-kew-roy) - Squirrel
Le chien (Luh shyehn) - Dog
Le chat (Luh shah) - Cat
La clôture (La clo-tew-ruh) - Fence
La voiture (La vwah-tew-ruh) - Car
Le camion (Luh cam-yohn) - Truck
La motocyclette (La mo-to-see-klet) - Motorcycle
La bicyclette (La bee-see-klet) - Cibyble
Le pôteau de téléphone (Luh po-to duh tay-lay-fonn) – Telephone pole
L'entrée (Lahn-tray) - Driveway
La rue (La rew) - Street
Le trottoir (Luh trot-wahr) - Sidewalk
La boîte postale (La bwaht poss-tal-uh) - Mailbox

Conversation #9: Want to play?

Concepts / vocabulary introduced:

Would you like to play?
Names of games and sports
Playground equipment

Preparation:

This one works best if you go to a playground and bring along some sports equipment.

The Conversation:

Explain to the student that they are going to pretend they have just met a new friend at the park and want to play with them. Have them practice the sentences a few times, then they should pretend you are their new friend and say "Salut! Veux-tu jouer? " (Sal-ew! Voo tew jhoo-ay?) They can then try asking what their new friend likes to do, and finally suggest an activity.

Salut! (Sal-ew!) - Hi
Veux-tu jouer ? (Voo tew jhoo-ay?) – Would you like to play ?
Aimes-tu XXX (Emm-tew XXX) – Do you like XXX ?
Je peux jouer aussi ? (Jhuh poo jhoo-ay oh-see?) – Can I play too ?
Nous allons jouer XXX (Noo zal-lohn jhoo-ay XXX) – L et's play XXX
Allons à (Al-lohn za XXX) – Let's go to XXX

Vocabulary:

Games:
Le tennis (Luh ten-neess) - Tennis
Le soccer (Luh sok-kair) - Soccer
Le basketball (Luh bass-ket-ball) - Basketball
Le baseball (Luh bayz-ball) - Baseball

Equipment:
La balançoire (La bal-ahn-swah-ruh) - Swing
La glissade (La glee-sad-uh) - Slide
Le carré de sable (Luh car-ray duh sah-bluh) - Sandbox
Le ballon (Luh bal-lohn) - Ball
Le cerf-volant (Luh sair vol-ahn) - Kits

Activities:
Marcher (Mar-shay) – to walk
Courir (Koo-reer) – to run
Sauter (So-tay) – to jump
Grimper (Grayhm-per) – to climb
Botter le ballon (Bot-tay luh bal-lohn) – to kick
Lancer (Lahn-say) – to throw
Courrons (Koor-ohn) – Let's run
Sautons (So-tohn) – Let's jump
Grimpons (Grayhm-pohn) – Let's climb
Jouons avec XXX (Jhoo-ohn a-vek XXX) – Let's play with XXX
Jouons sur XXX (Jhoo-ohn soor XXX) – Let's play on XXX

Conversation #10:   Ouch!

Concepts / vocabulary introduced:

Parts of the body

Preparation:

None needed

The Conversation:

Children usually have more fun with learning body parts if you can make it silly. For example, pretend to trip, and stand up holding part of your body and say "Aïe! Je me suis blessé le bras!" (I-ee! Juh muh swee bless-ay luh brah!). Then point to the arm, and say "le bras" (luh brah) and have your students repeat it while pointing to their own arm. You can also bring in an ice pack, and pretend to put it on the hurting spot, then pass it to the student.

You also can go over a few parts of the body with them, then say "Qu'est-ce que c'est?" (kes-kuh say) (What is this?) while pointing to a part of the body to test their knowledge.

And, finally here is a translation of the "hokey pokey" song you can sing. Stand in a circle, and substitute a body part for the __:

> Mets la main devant (may la mayhn duh vahn) (put the part inside the circle)

Mets la main derrière (may la mayhn dair-yair) (put the part outside the circle)

Mets la main devant (may la mayhn duh vahn) (put the part inside the circle)

Et remue-la dans tous les sens (ay ruh-mew la dahn too lay sahn) (shake the part inside the circle)

Tu fais le hokey pokey (tew fay luh hokey pokey)

Tu tournes sur toi-même (tew toor-nuh soor twa-mem) (turn in a circle)

Voilà c'est comme ça (vwa-lah say com sa) (clap your hands with this part)

Vocabulary:

Le bras (Luh brah) - arm
Le dos (Luh doe) - back
La colonne vertébrale (la col-on vair-tay-bral-uh) - backbone
Le cerveau (Luh sair-vo) - brain
La poitrine (La pwah-tree-nuh) - chest
Les fesses (Lay fess-uh) - buttocks
Le mollet (Luh moll-ay) - calf
L'oreille (Lor-ray-yuh) - ear
Le coude (Luh coo-duh) - elbow
L'œil (Loy) - eye
Le doigt (Luh dwah) - finger
Le pied (Luh pyay) - foot
Les cheveux (Lay shuh-voo) - hair
La main (La mayhn) - hand
La tête (La tet-tuh) - head
Le coeur (Luh coor) - heart
La hanche (La ahn-shuh) - hip
Le genou (Luh jhuh-noo) - knee
La jambe (La jhahm-buh) - leg
La bouche (La boo-shuh) - mouth

Le muscle (Luh mews-kluh) - muscle
Le cou (Luh coo) - neck
Le nez (Luh nay) - nose
L'épaule (Lay-pole-luh) - shoulder
La peau (La po) - skin
Le ventre (Luh vahn-truh) – stomach (abdomen)
La cuisse (La kwee-suh) - thigh
La gorge (La gor-jhuh) - throat
L'orteil (Lor-tay) - toe
La langue (La lahn-guh) - tongue
La dent (La dahn) - tooth

Conversation #11:   How was school today?

Concepts / vocabulary introduced:

Words relating to common school activities.

Preparation:

You will want to get a few props together relating to the activities you are going to ask about. For example, have a paint brush handy if you are going to ask about painting. Have a story book at hand to ask about reading.

The Conversation:

First you will ask, "Qu'est-ce que tu as fait à l'école aujourd'hui?" (Kess-kuh tew ah fay a lay-kol-luh o-jhoor-dwee?) - What did you do at school today?

Then, you will ask specific questions, while pretending to do the activity. There may be some cases which don't role play very well – then you can ask the question, then translate into English, then ask again.

For example, you might say "As-tu joué dehors? " (Ah-tew jhoo-ay duh-or?) - Did you play outside? The child might answer "Oui" (wee) or "Non" (no). Once they have answered, feed them the entire answer sentence in French – either "Oui, j'ai joué dehors" (Wee, jhay jhoo-ay duh-or) or "Non, je n'ai pas joué dehors" (No, jhuh nay pah jhoo-ay duh-or), and have them repeat it.

Vocabulary:

Here are question and possible answer combinations:

As-tu lu une histoire ? (Ah-tew lew ewn ee-stwah-ruh?) – Did you read a story?
Oui, j'ai lu une histoire. (Wee, jhay lew ewn ee-stwah-ruh.) – Yes, I read a story.
Non, je n'ai pas lu une histoire. (No, jhuh nay pah lew ewn ee-stwah-ruh.) – No, I did not read a story.

As-tu joué dehors? (Ah-tew jhoo-ay duh-or?) – Did you play outside ?
Oui, j'ai joué dehors. (Wee, jhay jhoo-ay duh-or.) – Yes, I played outside.
Non, je n'ai pas joué dehors. (No, jhuh nay pah jhoo-ay duh-or.) – No, I did not play outside.

As-tu joué avec XXX ? (Ah-tew jhoo-ay a-vek XXX?) – Did you play with XXX? (person's name)
Oui, j'ai joué avec XXX. (Wee, jhay jhoo-ay a-vek XXX.) – Yes, I played with XXX.
Non, je n'ai pas joué avec XXX. (No, jhuh nay pah jhoo-ay a-vek XXX.) – No, I did not play with XXX.

As-tu fait de la peinture? (Ah-tew fay duh la payhn-tew-ruh?) – Did you paint?
Oui, j'ai fait de la peinture. (Wee, jhay fay duh la payhn-tew-ruh.) – Yes, I painted.
Non, je n'ai pas fait de la peinture. (No, jhuh nay pah fay duh la payhn-tew-ruh.) – No, I did not paint.

As-tu colorié? (Ah-tew col-lor-yay?) – Did you color ?
Oui, j'ai colorié. (Wee jhay col-lor-yay.) – Yes, I colored.
Non, je n'ai pas colorié. (No, jhuh nay pah col-lor-yay.) – No, I did not color.

As-tu fait un dessin ? (Ah tew fay uhn des-sayhn?) – Did you draw a picture?
Oui, j'ai fait un dessin. (Wee, jhay fay uhn des-sayhn.) – Yes, I drew a picture.
Non, je n'ai pas fait un dessin. (No, jhuh nay pah fay uhn des-sayhn.) – No, I did not draw a picture.

As-tu écrit un test? (Ah-tew ay-kree uhn test?) – Did you take a test?

Oui, j'ai écrit un test. (Wee jhay ay-kree uhn test.) – Yes, I took a test.

Non, je n'ai pas écrit un test. (No, jhuh nay pah zay-kree uhn test.) – No, I did not take a test.

As-tu déjeûné? (Ah-tew day-jhuh-nay?) – Did you eat lunch ?

Oui, j'ai déjeûné. (Wee, jhay-day-jhuh-day.) – Yes, I ate lunch.

Non, je n'ai pas déjeûné. (No, jhay nay pas day-jheûn-nay.) – No, I did not eat lunch.

Timing of events:

You can also add some timing words to the end of your questions:

Aujourd'hui (o-jhoor-dwee) - today

Ce matin (suh ma-tayhn) – this morning

Cet après-midi (set ap-pray mee-dee) – this afternoon

Avant l'école (av-vahn lay-kol-luh) – before school

Pendant la récréation (pahn-dahn la ray-kray-ass-yohn) – during recess

Après l'école (ap-pray lay-kol-luh) – after school

Conversation #12:   Time for Dinner!

Concepts / vocabulary introduced:

Polite requests
Some food names
Plate, silverware, glass

Preparation:

Select and prepare a dinner with several choices in it. The vocabulary list in this role play is designed around steak, chicken, potatoes and vegetables. You may also need to look up a few ingredients, if you have different options than we use. Write down any items you offer that we don't include, and then go to Translate.Google.com, type in the word, and have it give you the French equivalent. Make a small cheat sheet for yourself if you need it.

To start, arrange your items on the counter ready to serve. Each person will need to select what they want and answer questions about each of the possible choices.

The Conversation:

First, when the family comes to dinner, say "Bienvenu au resto français!" (byehn-vuh-new o res-toe frahn-say)

Let them know that:

> J'aimerais (jhem-uh-ray) = I would like, a polite way of asking for something
>
> Aimerais-tu (em-uh-ray tew) = Would you like?

Oui (wee) = Yes

Non merci (no mair-see) = No thank you

Encore (ahn-kor) = More

Then for each person, stand by the ingredients holding their plate.

First, show the steak and chicken. Ask them, "Veux-tu du steak ou du poulet? " (Voo-tew dew stake oo dew poo-lay) while you hold up first the steak, then the chicken.

Once they have selected, put it on the plate.

Then go through the choices, and they answer yes or no to each.

For example, if you have green beans, ask "Veux-tu des haricots verts?" (Voo-tew day a-ree-ko vair ?)

They answer either "Oui, je veux des haricots verts. " (Wee, jhuh voo day a-ree-ko vair?), or "Non, merci, pas de haricots verts". (No, mair-see, pah duh ar-ee-ko vair)

 Once you put a spoonful on their plate, ask if they would like more: "Veux-tu encore des haricots verts?" (Voo-tu ahn-kor day a-ree-ko vair ?) And they can again answer, "Oui, j'aimerais encore des haricots verts. " (Wee, jhem-uh-ray ahn-kor day a-ree-ko vair), or "Non, merci. " (No, mair-see).

You may also ask if they would like a drink, "Veux-tu un XXX?" (Voo-tew uhn XXX)

They answer either "Oui, j'aimerais XXX. " (Wee, jhem-uh ray XXX), or "Non, merci, pas de XXX. " (No, mair-see, pah duh XXX).

<u>Vocabulary:</u>

Steak (stake) - steak
Poulet (poo-lay) - chicken
Pommes de terre rôties (pom duh tair ro-tee) – roasted potatoes
Pommes de terre pilées (pom duh tair pee-lay) – mashed potatoes
Haricots verts (a-ree-ko vair) – green beans
Carottes (ca-rot) - carrots
Sauce (so-suh) - gravy
Fromage (fro-majh-uh) - cheese
Fruit (frwee) - fruit
Lait (lay) - milk
Eau (oh) - water
Jus de pommes (jhew duh pom) – apple juice

Conversation #13:   Over, under, in, out

Concepts / vocabulary introduced:

Words describing location

Preparation:

You will need a toy (I use a bear in my examples), and a large box (big enough for you to step into).

The Conversation:

You will show the comparison using the bear or box, and then ask the child(ren) to imitate it, as they will learn much faster if they say it themselves.

Here are suggestions:

Lift up the bear, and say "L'ourson est en haut." (Loor-sohn et ahn oh) - (the bear is up). Put it down, and say "L'ourson est en bas. " (Loor-sohn et ahn bah) - (the bear is down).

Hold the bear over the box, and say "L'ourson est sur la boîte." (Loor-sohn ay soor la bwah-tuh) - (the bear is over the box). Then, lift up the box and hold the bear under it, and say "L'ourson est sous la boîte." (Loor-sohn ay soo la bwah-tuh) - (the bear is under the box).

Climb inside the box, and say "Je suis dans la boîte." (Jhuh swee dahn la bwah-tuh) - (I am inside the box). Then climb back out and say "Je suis en dehors de la boîte." (Jhuh swee zahn duh-or duh la bwah-tuh) - (I am outside the box).

Stand behind the box, and say "Je suis derrière la boîte." (Jhuh swee dair-yair la bwah-tuh) - (I am behind the box). Move to the side of it, and say "Je suis à côté de la boîte." (Jhuh swee za ko-tay duh la bwah-tuh) - (I am next to the box). Stand in front of it, and say "Je suis devant la boîte." (Jhuh swee duh-vahn la bwah-tuh) - (I am in front of the box).

Then, move on to questions: "Où est l'ourson?" (Oo ay loor-sohn) - (Where is the bear?).

Vocabulary:

En haut (Ahn oh) - Up
En bas (Ahn bah) - Down
Au dessus (Oh dess-ew) - Over
Sous (Soo) - Under
Dedans (Duh-dahn) - Inside
Dehors (Duh-or) - Outside
À côté (A ko-tay) – To the side
Derrière (Dair-yair-ruh) - Behind
Devant (Duh-vahn) – In front of

Conversation #14: Around the house

Concepts / vocabulary introduced:

Names of common household items

Preparation:

None needed.

The Conversation:

You will walk around the house, and point to or touch items and name them. Then, the child(ren) should imitate. Once you've named the object, describe it using some of the words from prior lessons.

For example, walk up to the wall, rap on it with your knuckles, and say "mur" (mewr). Once your students imitate that, describe the wall, for example "mur blanc" (mewr blahn) (white wall) and have them repeat.

Once you've covered the vocabulary, go around again, point to objects and say "Qu'est-ce que c'est?" (kess-kuh-say) – "What is this?" – to check what your students remember.

Vocabulary:

Le grenier (luh gruh-nyay) - attic
Le sous-sol (luh soo-sol) - basement
La salle de bain (la sal duh bayhn) - bathroom
La chambre à coucher (la shahm-bruh a coo-shay) - bedroom
La garde-robe (la gar-duh rob) - closet
La cour (la koor) - courtyard

Le bureau (luh bew-roh) – den, study
La salle à manger (la sal a mahn-jhay) – dining room
L'entrée (lahn-tray) - entryway
La salle de séjour (la sal duh say-jhoor) – family room
Le garage (luh ga-ra-jhuh) - garage
La cuisine (la kwee-zeen) - kitchen
Le salon (luh sa-lohn) – living room
La pièce (la pyess-uh) - room
Le plafond (luh plaf-ohn) - ceilint
Le cabinet (luh ca-bee-nay) - cabinet
La porte (la port) - door
La prise de courant (la preez duh coo-rahn) – electrical socket
Le robinet (luh rob-ee-nay) - faucet
Le plancher (luh plahn-shay) - floor
l'étage (lay-tajh-uh) - upstairs
Le comptoir de cuisine (luh cohm-twahr duh kwee-zeen) – kitchen counter
La lampe (la lahm-puh) - lamp
La lumière (la lew-myair-uh) - light
Le miroir (luh meer-wahr) = mirror
Le toît (luh twah) - roof
L'évier (lay-vyay) - sink
L'escalier (less-kal-yay) - stairs
Le mur (luh mewr) - wall
La fenêtre (la fuh-net-truh) - window
Le lit (luh lee) - bed
La chaise (la shayz-uh) - chair
La commode (la kom-mod-uh) – chest of drawers
Le sofa (luh so-fah) - sofa
La table (la tab-luh) - table

Conversation #15:   I spy

Concepts / vocabulary introduced:

This is a review of things you have worked on in prior lessons.

Preparation:

None needed.

The Conversation:

"Je vois quelque chose" (juh vwah kel-kuh shoze-uh) – I see something

Walk around the house, looking for items you've previously used in your role plays. Once you spot something, say "Je vois quelque chose" (juh vwah kel-kuh shoze-uh) – I see something – and then something about the item you are looking at. For example, if you see a train which is green, you would say "Je vois quelque chose de vert " (juh vwah kel-kuh shoze duh vair), and then the correct answer would be "un train" (uhn trayhn) – a train.

Some of the things you can look for are:

- Foods or dishes in the kitchen

- Clothing in the bedrooms

- Furniture items

- Toys

Activities

To play, look at the map and follow the directions. Once you solve these, make up your own to share! As a next step, get out a map of your city or country and write down directions for another person to solve.

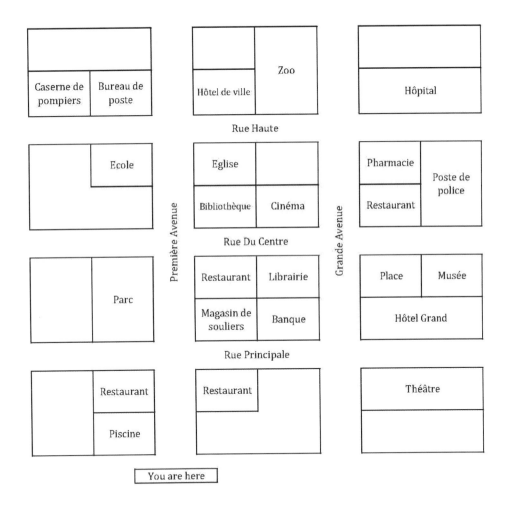

Route #1:

Directions:
Va tout droit. (vah too drwah)
Au deuxième coin de rue, tourne à droite. (o doo-zyem kwahn duh rew, toorn a drwah-tuh)
Va tout droit. (vah too drwah)
Au deuxième coin de rue, ta destination sera sur la droite. (au doo-zyem kwahn duh rew, ta dess-tee-na-syohn suh-ra soor la drwah-tuh)

Where did you end up?
Now, give directions to go from that location to the zoo.

Route #2:

Directions:
Va tout droit. (vah too drwah)
Au troisième coin de rue, ta destination sera de l'autre côté de la rue sur la gauche. (o trwa-zyem kwayhn duh rew, ta dess-tee-na-syohn suh-ra duh lo-truh ko-tay duh la rew soor la go-shuh)

Where did you end up?
Now, give directions to go from that location to the pharmacy.

Route #3:

Directions:
Va tout droit. (vah too drwah)
Au premier coin de rue, tourne à droite. (o pruh-myay kwahn duh rew, toor-nuh a drwah-tuh)
Va tout droit. (vah too drwah)
Au premier coin de rue, tourne à gauche. (o pruh-myay kwahn duh rew, toor-nuh a go-shuh)
Ta destination sera sur la gauche. (ta dess-tee-na-syohn suh-ra soor la go-shuh)

Where did you end up?
Now, give directions to go from that location to the police station.

Map Game Word List

Where is (the)...? Où est...?
It's...   Il est...

Locations:
La banque (la bahn-kuh) - bank
La salle de bain (la sal duh bayhn) - bathroom
La librairie (la lee-brair-ee) - bookstore
L'église (lay-gleez-uh) - churck
L'hôtel de ville (lo-tel duh vil) – city hall
La caserne de pompiers (la ka-zair-nuh duh pohm-pyay) – fire station
L'épicerie (lay-pee-suh-ree) – grocery store
L'hôpital (lop-ee-tal) -hospital
L'hôtel (lo-tel) - hotel
La bibliothèque (la bee-blee-o-tek) - library
Le cinéma (luh see-nay-mah) – movie theater
Le musée (luh mew-zay) - museum
Le parc (luh park) - park
La pharmacie (la far-ma-see) - pharmacy
Le poste de police (luh poss-tuh duh pol-ee-suh) – police station
Le bureau de poste (luh bew-ro duh poss-tuh) – post office
Le restaurant (luh rest-o-rahn) - restaurant
L'école (lay-kol-luh) - school
Le magasin de souliers (luh mag-a-zayhn duh soo-lyay) – shoe store
La piscine (la pee-seen) – swimming pool
Le théâtre (luh tay-ah-truh) - theater
Le zoo (luh zoh) - zoo

Distances, directions:
Kilomètre, mètre (kee-lo-may-truh, may-truh) – kilometer, meter
Rue, avenue, autoroute (rew, av-uh-new) – street, avenue, highway
Pâté de maisons (pah-tay duh may-zohn) – city block
Coin de rue (kwayhn duh rew) – street corner
Adresse (a-dress) - address
Tourne (toor-nuh) - turn

Fais demi-tour (fay duh-mee-toor) – turn around
Les feux de circulation (lay fuh duh seer-kew-la-syohn) – traffic lights
L'intersection (layhn-ter-sek-syohn) - intersection
La place (la plass-uh) – square or plaza
En face de (ahn fass duh) - opposite
Derrière (dair-yair) - behind
Devant (duh-vahn) – in front of
Sur cette rue (soor set rew) – along this street
A droite (a drwah-tuh) – on / to the right
A gauche (a go-shuh) – on / to the left
Va tout droit (vah too drwah) – go straight ahead
Au bout (o boo) – at / to the end
Jusqu'à (jhoos-ka) – up to / as far as
Au coin (o kwayhn) – at the corner
C'est sur (say soor) – Itis on / in
 Nord (nor) - North
Sud (sood) - South
Est (est) - East
Ouest (west) - West

1. Get several pieces of paper or index cards, and put together clues that lead from place to place.

2. Decide what the prize will be at the end of the hunt. It does not have to be anything fancy – the chance to go on the treasure hunt will be fun in itself – but a prize is fun, perhaps some stickers, or have it end at your car and take everyone to the park.

3. Hand your students the first clue, and see how they do! If your students do not read yet – walk with them and read each clue for them as they find it.

Here are some sample clues with translations.

Look under __'s bed	Regarde sous le lit de ___ (ruh-gar-duh soo luh lee duh ___)
Look under __'s pillow	Regarde sous l'oreiller de ___ (ruh-gar-duh soo lor-ay-yay duh___)
Look inside the refrigerator	Regarde dans le réfrigérateur (ruh-gar-duh dahn luh ray-free-jhay-rat-oor)
Look where we keep the milk	Regarde où nous gardons le lait (ruh-gar-duh oo noo gar-dohn luh lay)
Look in the bathroom	Regarde dans la salle de bain (ruh-gar-duh dahn la sal duh bayhn)
Look in the bathtub	Regarde dans le bain (ruh-gar-duh dahn luh bayhn)

Look under the bathroom rug	Regarde sous le tapis de bain (ruh-gar-duh soo luh tap-ee duh bayhn)
Look under the sofa	Regarde sous le sofa (ruh-gar-duh soo luh so-fah)
Look next to the red chair	Regarde à côté de la chaise rouge (ruh-gar-duh a ko-tay duh la shayz-uh roo-jhuh)
Look at the kitchen table	Regarde la table de cuisine (ruh-gar-duh la tab-luh duh kwee-zeen)
Look in your top dresser drawer	Regarde dans le premier tiroir de ta commode (ruh-gar-duh dahn luh pruhm-yay tee-rwahr duh ta kom-mod)
Look inside __'s closet	Regarde dans la garde-robe de ___ (ruh-gar-duh dahn la gar-duh-rob duh ___)
Look under the kitchen sink	Regarde sous l'évier de cuisine (ruh-gar-duh soo lay-vyay)
Look under the bathroom sink	Regarde sous le lavabo (ruh-gar-duh soo luh lav-a-bo)
Look on __'s desk	Regarde sur le bureau de ___ (ruh-gar-duh soor luh bew-ro duh ___)
Look above the fireplace	Regarde sur le manteau de cheminée (ruh-gar-duh soor luh mahn-toe duh shuh-mee-nay)
Look inside the dishwasher	Regarde dans le lave-vaisselle (ruh-gar-duh dahn luh lav-vess-ell)

Look near the front door	Regarde près de la porte avant (ruh-gar-duh pray duh la port a-vahn)
Look near the garage door	Regarde près de la porte de garage (ruh-gar-duh pray duh la port duh ga-rajh-uh)
Look in the laundry room	Regarde dans la salle de lavage (ruh-gar-duh dahn la sal duh la-vajh-uh)
Look near the car	Regarde près de la voiture (ruh-gar-duh pray duh la vwah-tew-ruh)
Look at the top of the stairs	Regarde en haut de l'escalier (ruh-gar-duh ahn-o duh less-kal-yay)
Look at the bottom of the stairs	Regarde en bas de l'escalier (ruh-gar-duh ahn bah duh less-kal-yay)
Look in the hall closet	Regarde dans le placard du passage (ruh-gar-duh dahn luh plak-ar dew pass ajh-uh)
Look on top of the refrigerator	Regarde sur le réfrigérateur (ruh-gar-duh soor luh ray-free-jhay-rat-oor)
Look near your shoes	Regarde près de tes souliers (ruh-gar-duh pray duh tay sool-yay)

Scavenger Hunt #1

Try to find each of the following items:

Epingle de sûreté (ay-payhn-gluh duh soo-ruh-tay)

Trombone (trom-bon-uh)

Clé (clay)

Livre (lee-vruh)

Disque compact (disc cohm-pact)

Mouchoir (moosh-wahr)

Téléphone (tay-lay-fon-uh)

Enveloppe (ahn-vuh-lop-uh)

Timbre (tayhm-bruh)

Bande élastique (bahn-day-lass-teek)

Journal (jhoor-nal)

Magazine (mag-a-zeen-uh)

Photographie (fo-toe-graf-ee)

Boîte (bwah-tuh)

Stylo (stee-lo)

Try to find each of the following items:

Brosse à dents (bross a dahn)

Brosse à cheveux (bross a shuh-voo)

Crayon (cray-ohn)

Pince à cheveux (payhn-s a shuh-voo)

Colle (kol-luh)

Pinceau (payhn-so)

Chaussette (sho-set-tuh)

Soulier (sool-yay)

Poupée (poo-pay)

Petite voiture (puh-teet-uh vwah-tew-ruh)

Animal en peluche (a-nee-mal ahn puh-lewsh-uh)

Crayon de couleur (cray-ohn duh coo-loor)

Ciseaux (see-zo)

Ruban adhésif (rew-bahn a-day-zeef)

Ballon (bal-lohn)

Try to find each of the following items:

Chemise (shuh-meez-uh)

Chapeau (shap-o)

Cuiller (kwee-air)

Fourchette (foor-shet-tuh)

Tasse (tahss-uh)

Tasse à mesurer (tahss a muh-zew-ray)

Petit bol (puh-tee bol)

Craquelin (cra-kuh-layhn)

Fruit (frwee)

Feuille (foy-uh)

Fleur (floor)

Brin d'herbe (brayhn dair-buh)

Petite roche (puh-tee-tuh rosh-uh)

Petite pelle (puh-tee-tuh pell-uh)

Sceau (so)

#1:

Epingle de sûreté (ay-payhn-gluh duh soo-ruh-tay)	safety pin
Trombone (trom-bon-uh)	paper clip
Clé (clay)	key
Livre (lee-vruh)	book
Disque compact (disc cohm-pact)	CD
Mouchoir (moosh-wahr)	tissue
Téléphone (tay-lay-fon-uh)	telephone
Enveloppe (ahn-vuh-lop-uh)	envelope
Timbre (tayhm-bruh)	stamp
Bande élastique (bahn-day-lass-teek-uh)	rubber band
Journal (jhoor-nal)	newspaper
Magazine (mag-a-zeen-uh)	magazine
Photographie (fo-toe-graf-ee)	photograph
Boîte (bwah-tuh)	box
Stylo (stee-lo)	pen

#2:

Brosse à dents (bross a dahn)	toothbrush
Brosse à cheveux (bross a shuh-voo)	hairbrush
Crayon (cray-ohn)	pencil
Pince à cheveux (payhn-sa shuh-voo)	hair clip
Colle (kol-luh)	glue
Pinceau (payhn-so)	paintbrush
Chaussette (sho-set-tuh)	sock
Soulier (sool-yay)	shoe
Poupée (poo-pay)	doll
Petite voiture (puh-teet-uh vwah-tew-ruh)	toy car
Animal en peluche (a-nee-mal ahn puh-lewsh-uh)	stuffed animal
Crayon de couleur (cray-ohn duh coo-loor)	crayon
Ciseaux (see-zo)	scissors
Ruban adhésif (rew-bahn a-day-zeef)	tape
Ballon (bal-lohn)	ball

#3:

Chemise (shuh-meez-uh)	shirt
Chapeau (shap-o)	hat
Cuiller (kwee-air)	spoon
Fourchette (foor-shet-tuh)	fork
Tasse (tahss-uh)	cup
Tasse à mesurer (tahss a muh-zew-ray)	measuring cup
Petit bol (puh-tee bol)	small bowl
Craquelin (cra-kuh-layhn)	cracker
Fruit (frwee)	fruit
Feuille (foy-uh)	leaf
Fleur (floor)	flower
Brin d'herbe (brayhn dair-buh)	blade of grass
Petite roche (puh-tee-tuh rosh-uh)	small rock
Petite pelle (puh-tee-tuh pell-uh)	small shovel
Sceau (so)	bucket

Bingo

To play bingo you can make up cards in advance, or you can have the players make their own cards as a first step.

Create a blank card template and a list of vocabulary words – at least 8 for a 3 x 3 card, 16 for a 4 x 4 card, or 24 for a 5 x 5 card. Pass out a vocabulary list and each person can write in their choice of words in the squares on their card – no blank spaces or repeated words.

To play, call out vocabulary words and the players mark off that word on their card. In traditional bingo the first person to get a complete row, column, or corner to corner line completed wins. In blackout bingo the first person to mark off all their squares wins.

Games

This is a great game to use to reinforce the name of different body parts.

Here is the song in French; stand in a circle, and substitute a body part for the __:

> Mets la main devant (may la mayhn duh vahn) (put the part inside the circle)
>
> Mets la main derrière (may la mayhn dair-yair) (put the part outside the circle)
>
> Mets la main devant (may la mayhn duh vahn) (put the part inside the circle)
>
> Et remue-la dans tous les sens (ay ruh-mew la dahn too lay sahn) (shake the part inside the circle)
>
> Tu fais le hokey pokey (tew fay luh hokey pokey)
>
> Tu tournes sur toi-même (tew toor-nuh soor twa-mem) (turn in a circle)
>
> Voilà c'est comme ça (vwa-lah say com sa) (clap your hands with this part)

And, some body parts you can use:

Le bras (Luh brah) - arm
Le dos (Luh doe) - back
La colonne vertébrale (la col-on vair-tay-bral-uh) - backbone
Le cerveau (Luh sair-vo) - brain

La poitrine (La pwah-tree-nuh) - chest
Les fesses (Lay fess-uh) - buttocks
Le mollet (Luh moll-ay) - calf
L'oreille (Lor-ray-yuh) - ear
Le coude (Luh coo-duh) - elbow
L'œil (Loy) - eye
Le doigt (Luh dwah) - finger
Le pied (Luh pyay) - foot
Les cheveux (Lay shuh-voo) - hair
La main (La mayhn) - hand
La tête (La tet-tuh) - head
Le coeur (Luh coor) - heart
La hanche (La ahn-shuh) - hip
Le genou (Luh jhuh-noo) - knee
La jambe (La jhahm-buh) - leg
La bouche (La boo-shuh) - mouth
Le muscle (Luh mews-kluh) - muscle
Le cou (Luh coo) - neck
Le nez (Luh nay) - nose
L'épaule (Lay-pole-luh) - shoulder
La peau (La po) - skin
Le ventre (Luh vahn-truh) – stomach (abdomen)
La cuisse (La kwee-suh) - thigh
La gorge (La gor-jhuh) - throat
L'orteil (Lor-tay) - toe
La langue (La lahn-guh) - tongue
La dent (La dahn) - tooth

Concentration

To play concentration, you will need a set of cards with 2 cards for each specific picture or word. You lay the cards upside down, and turn over 2 at a time. If the 2 match – you keep them. If not, you turn them back over and the next person gets their turn. If you pay close attention you will be able to remember where some items are as you go along, increasing your matches. The quickest way to begin playing is to purchase 2 identical sets of French flash cards and shuffle them together.

To reinforce French vocabulary, instead of having 2 matching cards – have sets of a picture and the name of that item in French, or sets with the word in French on one card and in English on the other. Then, you need to remember the vocabulary to get a match. Start with a list of vocabulary words you'd like to practice, and write the French and English words on index cards.

Où est... ?

Où est... ? (oo ay) means, "Where is?". This can be used around the house by naming specific objects or rooms, or outside by naming types of buildings or other items you might see, like a tree or bench.

Qu'est-ce que c'est ?

Qu'est-ce que c'est ? (kess-kuh-say) means, "What is this?" It's good for pointing at objects to see if others can correctly name them in French. Use it with objects around the house or body parts. I have a friend who has taped index cards to various items in her house to help her remember them – "la porte" on the door for example – you may want to try this as well!

Twister

Twister can be played with a twister board from the game, or you can make your own playing area by placing colored pieces of paper on the ground. To play, one person calls out the instructions which the others follow. You can use a twister spinner to select them, or assign numbers on a pair of dice (one represents color, one represents body part), or just call out what you like! The last one to fall over wins!

Example calls:

Mets ta main droite sur la couleur bleu. (May ta mayhn drwah-tuh soor la coo-loor bloo) – put your right hand on the color blue

Mets ton pied gauche sur la couleur orange. (May tohn pyay go-shuh soor la coo-loor or-ahn-jhuh) – put your left foot on the color orange

Words you may need:

Gauche (go-shuh) - Left
Droite (drwah-tuh) - Right
Main (mayhn) - Hand
Pied (pyay) - Foot
Tête (tet-uh) - Head
Rouge (roo-jhuh) - Red
Orange (or-ahn-jhuh) - Orange
Jaune (jho-nuh) - Yellow
Vert (vair) - Green
Bleu (bloo) - Blue
Noir (nwahr) - Black
Blanc (blahn) - White

A fun game to play with children is similar to charades. Each person takes a turn pretending to be an animal. The person who correctly guesses the animal and names it in French gets to go next!

Here's a list of animal names to get you started:

L'élan (lay-lahn) - moose
Le cheval (luh shuh-val) - horse
Le chameau (luh sham-o) - camel
Le kangourou (luh kahn-goo-roo) - kangaroo
Le zèbre (luh zeb-ruh) - zebra
Le cochon (luh cosh-ohn) - pig
Le chimpanzé (luh shayhm-pahn-zay) - chimpanzee
Le cerf (luh sairf) - der
Le lapin (luh la-payhn) - rabbit
L'éléphant (lay-lay-fahn) - elephant
Le phoque (luh fok-uh) - seal
Le chat (luh shah) - cat
Le gorille (luh gor-ee-yuh) - gorilla
Le guépard (luh gay-par) - cheetah
La giraffe (la jhee-raf-uh) - giraffe
L'hippopotame (lee-po-po-tam-uh) - hippopotamus
Le koala (luh ko-a-lah) - koala
Le lion (luh lyohn) - lion
L'otarie (lot-a-ree) – sea lion
Le léopard (luh lay-o-par) - leopard
Le singe (luh sayhn-jhuh) - monkey
L'ours (loorss) - bear
Le chien (luh shyehn) - dog
Le rhinocéros (luh ree-noss-ay-ross) - rhinoceros
Le tigre (luh tee-gruh) - tiger
Le renard (luh ruh-nar) - fox

Recommended additional materials

None of these items are necessary, however we have found them to be fun!

Songs for the car:

We enjoyed the "Teach Me French" CDs. They include songs about everyday activities, so they are a great way to practice your French, pick up a few new words, and have fun all at once!

Children's story books in French:

Simple children's books will have commonly used words and pictures to help with understanding, and are a great complement to the role plays. Check out what's available in your local library!

Children's DVDs with a French track:

Check your DVDs – I have a few with a French track. You can also purchase French children's DVDs from online from a French language store. Please keep in mind that DVDs originating from Europe will require a multi-region DVD player.

17701162R00046

Made in the USA
Lexington, KY
23 September 2012